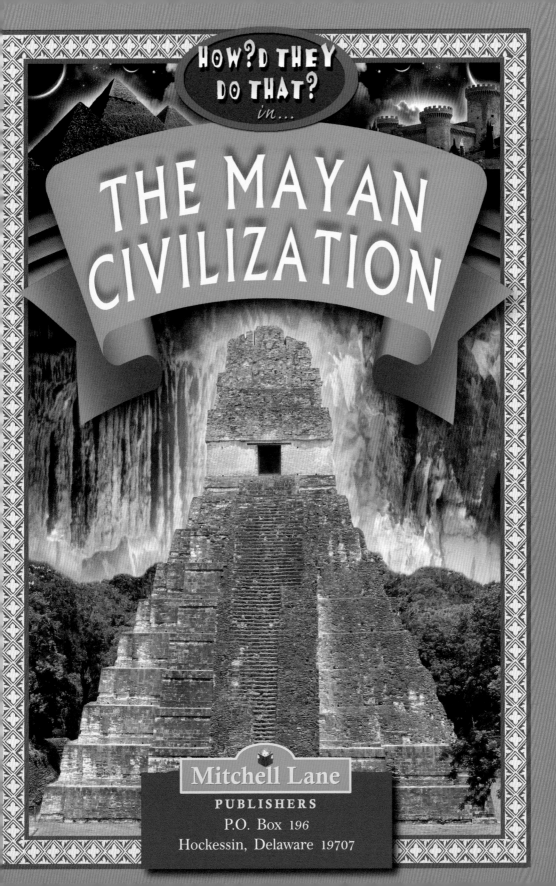

HOW?D THEY DO THAT?

in...

THE MAYAN CIVILIZATION

Mitchell Lane

PUBLISHERS

P.O. Box 196

Hockessin, Delaware 19707

HOW?D THEY DO THAT? in...

Ancient Egypt

Ancient Greece

Ancient Mesopotamia

Ancient Rome

The Aztec Empire

Colonial America

Elizabethan England

The Mayan Civilization

The Persian Empire

Pre-Columbian America

ELIZABETH SCHOLL

THE MAYA AREA

N
W   E
S

● **Modern Cities**
● **Archaeological Sites**

● **Mérida**
YUCATÁN
● Chichén
Itzá

● Uxmal
● Sayil

● Tulum

*QUINTANA
ROO*

CAMPECHE

TABASCO

MEXICO

● **Villahermosa**

● Palenque

Uaxactún ●

● Altun
Ha

● Tikal

BELIZE

● Toniná

● Yaxchilán

Caracol
●

● Bonampak

● Seibal

CHIAPAS

GUATEMALA

Quiriguá ●

● Copan

**Guatemala
City** ●

HONDURAS

EL SALVADOR

	Kilometers
0 25 50 100 150 200	

	Miles
0 25 50 100 150 200	

Mitchell Lane
PUBLISHERS

Printing   1   2   3   4   5   6   7   8   9

Library of Congress Cataloging-in-Publication Data
Scholl, Elizabeth J.
  How'd they do that in the Mayan civilization / by Elizabeth Scholl.
      p. cm. — (How'd they do that)
  Includes bibliographical references and index.
  ISBN 978-1-58415-822-6 (library bound)
 1. Mayas—Juvenile literature. 2. Mayas—Social life and customs—Juvenile literature.
3. Mayas—Intellectual life—Juvenile literature. 4. Mexico—Civilization—Juvenile
literture. 5. Central America—Civilization—Juvenile literature. I. Title.
  F1435.S338 2010
  972.81'016—dc22

                                                                        2009027330

PUBLISHER'S NOTE: This story is based on the author's extensive research, which she believes to be accurate. Documentation of such research is contained on page 60.

     To reflect current usage, we have chosen to use the secular era designations BCE ("before the common era") and CE ("of the common era") instead of the traditional designations BC ("before Christ") and AD (*anno Domini,* "in the year of the Lord").

     The internet sites referenced herein were active as of the publication date. Due to the fleeting nature of some web sites, we cannot guarantee they will all be active when you are reading this book.
                                                                        PLB

CONTENTS

Pacal and Zafrina sat atop the stone wall of the Grand Ball Court, waiting excitedly for the pregame ceremonies to begin. For Zafrina, the music and pageant before the game were not to be missed—in fact, they were almost as exciting as the game itself, and not nearly as scary.

It was a humid day at Chichén Itzá, but the heat of the midday sun did not deter the thousands of fans who crowded around the ball court. The ones who had arrived early enough, like Pacal and Zafrina and their family, had climbed the stone steps to get seats along the top of the walls that surrounded the playing field. These spots would give them the best view of the game and the ceremonies. Other people gathered around behind them, and some were able to see the court from other places in the city.

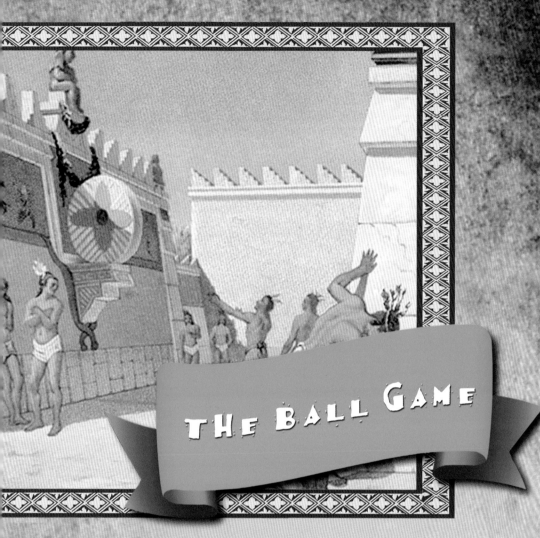

THE BALL GAME

Musicians began to play—some played drums and maracas, while others played flutes and ocarinas. Several players began to blow conch shells, which sounded like trumpets.

The players entered the ball court, costumed in colorful feather headdresses, animal skins, face paint and masks, stone yokes decorated with *palmas,* and *hachas* carved into animal shapes. They wore wristbands and anklets made from beads and shells, as well as jade necklaces.

The game did not begin until the players of both teams made offerings and prayed to the gods. One of the most important offerings the team could make was the captain's own blood. It was not a surprise, then, nor did it seem unusual to Zafrina and Pacal, when the shaman pierced the tongues of the team captains with a shark's tooth. The tongues were bled onto paper and burned, the smoke rising to the realm of the gods. After this ceremony, the game began.

The players on the two teams reentered the ball court. This time, their ceremonial costumes were gone, and instead they wore loincloths with a padded fabric yoke around their waists, instead of the stone one used for the opening ceremony. On their hips were leather hip guards. They wore knee and shin protectors, padded leg guards, padded arm bands, helmets, and padding for their private parts. The players also wore masks, which protected their faces.

The shaman entered the center of the court, offered a blessing, and started the game by throwing the hard rubber ball three times. The game began. The crowd cheered wildly as the players hit the ball with their hips, elbows, shoulders, and knees. In the Mayan ball game, the use of hands and feet was not allowed.

The object of the game was to get the ball through the goal, a stone ring that was attached to the walls on either side of the court. Because they couldn't use their hands or feet, and because the goal was so high, scoring was difficult.

Pacal and Zafrina, along with the other fans, from small children to grandparents, cheered and yelled when their team hit the ball back, and laughed at some of the funny positions the players used to hit the ball. Because scoring a goal was such a rare occurrence, the players spent most of the game trying to keep the ball in play. They couldn't let it bounce more than twice before hitting it back to the other team's side of the court.

The rubber ball was heavy, and getting hit by it could cause serious injuries. Zafrina didn't like to watch when a player got hit in the face and had to be carried off the field, but Pacal thought he would like to be brave enough to play the game when he grew up, and wouldn't be afraid of getting hurt.

When the game ended, Pacal and Zafrina's village's team had won. "Thank the gods," Zafrina thought, as she watched the stadium break out into chaos. It was customary for the winning team and its fans to take the clothing of the losing team and its fans. People held on to

The ornate headdresses of the ballplayers were often decorated with animals or gods, as well as the feathers of the quetzal, a bird that was sacred to the Mayas. Players on the winning team may have exchanged their leather or cloth yokes for stone ones during celebratory ceremonies.

A modern game called ulama, descended from the ancient Mayan ball game, is played in parts of Mexico. Played by two teams on a court drawn in the dirt, a point is scored when the opposing team misses the ball, hits the ball out of turn, touches the ball with a body part other than the hip, touches a teammate, or when the ball goes out of bounds or stops moving before it reaches the line in the center of the court.

their clothes and tried to run home, while the winners chased them, trying to grab the garments they felt were rightfully theirs.

Zafrina and Pacal walked back to their family's hut, recapping the exciting moments of the game. Thankfully, in today's game, only clothing was sacrificed. In some games, the captain of the losing team had his head cut off.

Ancient and Modern Sports

We may never discover the details of the ancient Mayan ball game, but many aspects of modern sporting events linger from that time. The rulers of ancient Mayan cities and towns spent a lot of money and resources and employed many workers building ball courts to impress the rulers and people of other towns, and to let them know that the city was wealthy and powerful. Modern towns and cities also spend large amounts on sports arenas. Sometimes they demolish old ones to build newer and better ones to attract more fans and sports teams.

Today, large groups of devoted fans travel to games by car, bus, and train, though many more stay home and watch the games on television. Of course, Mayans couldn't watch games on TV, so they had to travel to see ball games—and they had only their feet to get them there.

Today's rivalry among sports teams and fans of different towns or cities is nothing new, either. The teams from Mayan towns and cities had devoted fans, too, and there was a great deal of rivalry between players and fans of different places. Ball games were even believed to have been used as a method of settling disputes between towns and cities. And just as many people do today, the Mayas gambled on the outcome of ball games, sometimes betting large amounts of valuables, and sometimes more than they could afford. There were Mayas who made money on arranging bets for the games, just as people do today (though in many places it is illegal to be a bookie, or a person who takes bets and pays winnings depending on the outcome of an event). Just as celebrities often attend sports events today as spectators, important rulers, priests, and government officials frequented the ancient Mayan games.

Sports gear was as important to the Mayas as it is to today's players. Some parts of the uniforms were designed to protect the body, while certain aspects of the uniforms, such as the ceremonial costumes the Mayan players wore, were decorative as well.

Mayan ballplayer with three-part yoke and bird headdress, c. 650–850 CE

Palenque is the Spanish name for a Mayan city in Mexico. The four-story tower in the palace is the only one of its kind found at any Mayan site. Palenque's rulers were honored as divine beings. Some had deformed features such as enlarged skulls or extra fingers and toes, which were regarded as godlike.

WHO WERE THE MAYAS?

Chapter 1

Mayan civilization developed and flourished in the countries we now know as Mexico, Guatemala, Belize, Honduras, and El Salvador. The Mayas were not one large group of people, but many smaller groups that established individual villages, cities, cultures, and societies in the region. In fact, they did not call themselves *Mayas* at all. The various groups of Native Americans are grouped together under the name Maya because they share a similar language, though there were at least 31 distinct yet related Mayan languages that had developed by the time the Europeans arrived. We do not know what the Mayas called themselves.

Mayan art and architecture, two of the major achievements of the ancient Mayan civilization, varied according to specific area, yet were similar enough in style and technique to be grouped together under the Mayan name.

The Mayan culture originated around 2600 BCE, when Mayan people moved to the Yucatán area of Mexico from the west. The Mayas were not the first civilization in the area; the Olmecs had already established a civilization there earlier, and by interacting with the Olmecs, the Mayas developed their calendar, study of astronomy, system of writing, and rituals, including the Mesoamerican ball game.

The history of the ancient Mayan civilization is usually divided into three periods. The earliest period, referred to as the Pre-Classic period, began around 1800 BCE, and lasted until about 250 CE. The Mayan Classic period, from 250 to 900 CE, is regarded as the peak of Mayan Civilization—in terms of artistic accomplishment, highly developed societies with people in different classes and with specialized professions, and significant development in scientific and mathematical thinking. The Post-Classic period lasted from about 900 to 1500 CE. During this time, Mayas migrated to the Yucatán peninsula in Mexico. Before the Spanish conquered the area, various groups were waging war on one another, fighting for land. Though the ruins of many Mayan cities are from this period, the art and architecture of this time are not considered as great as that of the Classic Mayan period.

Over 4,000 years, the Mayan civilization grew, flourished, and declined. Historians who study the Mayas, known as Mayanists, aren't sure what actually happened, but evidence shows that there were probably multiple causes for the collapse of the Mayan civilization. There may have been a drought, causing a food shortage, or polluted water may have led to sickness and disease.

The ancient Mayan civilization finally fell when it was conquered by the Spanish, who began to explore in the area around 1500. Christopher Columbus encountered a group of Mayas in a canoe near Cuba, in 1503. Several years later, a Spanish ship was wrecked off the coast of Cozumel, an island that was sacred to the Mayas. The Spanish were captured and some were sacrificed by the Mayas. Before long, the Spanish had established colonies and began to invade Mayan cities. The battle raged on for twenty years, and the Mayas were eventually defeated. While many Mayas were killed in battle, many more died from the diseases the Europeans brought to the area. In their attempt to convert the Mayas to Christianity and European ways, the Spanish burned nearly all the Mayas' religious books. Because of this, there are many unanswered questions about the Mayan civilization.

Tikal in northern Guatemala is one of the largest Mayan cities that has been discovered. Temple I, also known as the Temple of the Great Jaguar, consists of nine levels of limestone. Some historians believe the nine levels may symbolize the nine Lords of the Night from Mayan mythology. Jasaw Chan K'awiil I, a famous ruler of Tikal, is buried in the Temple of the Great Jaguar.

Before the demise of their civilization, the Mayas developed a very sophisticated culture, with highly advanced systems of hieroglyphic writing, and a mathematical system that included two types of calendars (one of them measured time into the future as far as 2012) and the use of a symbol for zero. They also were expert astronomers. Even though they had no metal tools or the wheel, they were remarkably skillful builders of huge stone temples and pyramids. The Mayas also were advanced in trade, spirituality, agriculture, food preparation, and government.

The Mayas did not disappear after the Spanish conquest. In fact, six million Mayan people live in the modern Yucatán, Campeche, Quintana Roo, Tabasco, and Chiapas areas of Mexico, as well as in the Central American countries of Honduras, El Salvador, Guatemala, and Belize. Many speak Mayan as their primary language and maintain some of the traditions of their ancestors, while others have assimilated into the mainstream part of the culture, speaking Spanish or English as their primary language. Most are Christians, though some practice the Mayan religion. Some practice both.

Modern Mayan people

Mayan Language

In very ancient times, before 2000 BCE, there was one Mayan language spoken. As the Mayan people gradually moved to different areas, their languages changed, and as each group split from others, the languages became more and more diverse. Today, 31 Mayan languages are spoken by millions of people in Mexico, Guatemala, and Belize.

Between 400 and 300 BCE, three Mayan groups developed written languages. They used symbols known as glyphs to write words, phrases, and sentences. Mayan writing isn't read as we read words on a page. The glyphs are in pairs, and form columns from top to bottom. The reader reads each pair, from left to right, then goes down to read the following pair, and so on. When one reaches the bottom of a column, he or she goes to the top of the next column.

Most Mayas did not know how to read or write. There were Mayan scribes, and it is believed that both sons and daughters of rulers and other important families learned the scribal arts at special schools.

Mayan glyphs appear on many ancient artifacts, from gigantic stone stelae to tiny pieces of jewelry, like ear plugs. Mayan writing has been found carved into jade objects such as masks and belt decorations, in clay pottery, on the wooden beams of doorways, on the walls of caves, and on shells and bones.

Mayanists estimate that Mayas had thousands of books called codices, though today only

Mayan Palenque glyphs

four Mayan books remain. Franciscan Bishop Diego de Landa, who was responsible for burning all the Mayan books in 1562 in an attempt to stop the Mayas from practicing their religion and convert them to Christianity, described them: "They wrote their books on a large sheet doubled several times. This closed together between two boards which were highly decorated. They wrote on both sides of the sheet in columns, following the folds; and the paper they made from the roots of a tree, giving it a white gloss on which it was easy to write."[1]

First constructed in the fourth century BCE, Tikal was one of the most powerful kingdoms of the ancient Maya. It covered an area of about six square miles, and had as many as 3,000 structures. It is not known exactly how many people lived there, but Mayanists have estimated it may have been as many as 90,000.

MAYAN CITIES AND TOWNS

Chapter 2

Architecture in Mayan cities is one of the most astounding aspects of the ancient Mayan civilization. The extensive building projects indicate that the Mayas had a complex society and government, for it would have been impossible for them to carry out the building projects, with large numbers of workers and materials, without an organized system of government and management. Historians believe that there were bosses who supervised the builders, as well as managers in charge of obtaining, transporting, and preparing building materials.

In the early days of the Mayan civilization, buildings were not as elaborate as the later stone complexes. The early structures were rect-angular or oval thatched huts, supported by poles. They later evolved to clay and adobe buildings, and eventually to limestone.

The remarkable feat of building stone pyramids, temples, palaces, and ball courts required money as well as supplies and labor. Kings and queens commissioned the building projects, and architects and city planners were employed as supervisors. Some of these people were hired from other places, likely because of their expertise in the field, and brought to the city where the building would take place.

The architects and city planners supervised masons and plasterers for the actual building constructions, as well as sculptors and scribes for decorating the buildings and surrounding structures. Mayan cities were designed as complexes, connected by stone-and-plaster roads and stairways.

The most impressive and elaborate complexes were built during the Classic period, but the largest complexes in history were built earlier, in the late Pre-Classic period. El Mirador, in Guatemala, is believed to have consisted of 26 major cities, and about 60 smaller ones. By the Post-Classic period, smaller structures built with less detail and care had replaced the massive structures of the earlier periods.

Generally, cities consisted of large open plazas, which served as performance spaces for the public. Events such as religious ceremonies, dances, and ball games were held in these plazas. Huge buildings surrounded them, including stone pyramids, temples, and palaces, as well as ball courts and baths. Each was constructed to impress the people of the city as well as outsiders.

Temples were built on platforms and had the highest pyramids in the city. There were several rooms for prayer and ceremony, and shrines were constructed in niches in walls. Small rooms called *waybill* or *pilma* were considered rooms where gods or ancestors resided, or were they could be called into attendance during rituals. While some rituals took

Large-scale construction projects such as cities or the building of canals may have utilized as many as 10,000 workers. The architecture included soaring pyramids and round buildings that required arches.

Mayapan

Mayan sweat baths were used for health and spiritual purposes rather than for cleanliness. In Piedras Negras, a Mayan site in northwestern Guatemala, at least eight of these baths were found, many with dressing rooms and lounge areas.

place inside the temples, large ceremonies took place on the outdoor plazas, as the rooms were small and designed to hold only a small, probably elite group of people.

Palaces of lesser nobility were farther removed from the public space. Cities were often surrounded by farmland and forests, which provided the city's population with food. Common people lived farther away from the city, but often near a person of mid-rank authority. Houses, like the larger palace complexes, were also built as complexes for an extended family. A number of houses were built around a courtyard area, which often had a garden with fruit trees, chilies, and other plants. Within the living complex were separate buildings for living and storage, covered work areas for men, kitchens where women worked, and sometimes a steam bath area. Women also worked at weaving and pottery-making on covered porches.

FYInfo

Travel Between Mayan Cities

Causeways called *sacbeob*, meaning "white roads," were raised roads covered with cement made from white lime. The *sacbeob* connected various areas within Mayan cities, and also connected towns and cities. Some archaeologists believe the roads were used for military purposes, as armies could travel quickly along them; perhaps they were also used as trade routes. The longest known *sacbe*, in the northern Yucatán in Mexico, was 62 miles long. Where there were no *sacbeob*, Mayas traveled along trails. They had neither the wheel nor pack animals, so transportation between cities and towns via cart or carriage did not exist.

When they traveled on foot, the Mayas carried their belongings in net backpacks, with a strap around the pack and across their forehead. This effectively distributed the weight of their load. Mayas continue to use this method of transport.

Mayas also traveled to other cities by water in canoes. These were made from hollowed-out tree trunks and had a canopy made from palm leaves to shade the passengers from the hot sun. These were not the canoes we think of; they were as wide as 8 feet, and had up to 25 people rowing them. Because they were so large, they could be used for transporting goods for trade. Moving large, heavy items such as stone and wooden objects by canoe would have been much easier than carrying them on foot.

Mayas bought and sold a variety of goods in the marketplaces of cities and towns. It is believed that nearly all Mayan groups attended markets. Stone beads, shells, cotton cloth, salt, and cacao beans were used as money. The barter system was also used: People would exchange surplus goods they had, such as crops or pottery, for other goods they needed or wanted. According to Diego de Landa, "In the markets, they traded every manner of thing found in that land."[2]

Mayan sacbe in Yucatán, Mexico

Common Mayan houses were often built of wood and palm leaves, which stayed cool even in hot weather. While the men were in the fields, the women and young children would work near the home preparing food, tending the gardens, weaving cloth, and making clothes.

FAMILY LIFE

Chapter 3

Ancient Mayan civilizations were generally divided into two classes: nobles and commoners (though there may have been a middle class as well). Most people stayed within the class into which they were born, and their class determined their career path. However, there were two ways a man could raise his social class. One was to become a warrior, and be good at it. Another was to train to be a priest, though higher-level priests were generally born into more elite families.

Within the classes, there were different types of positions. Nobles ranged from the most important position as king or queen to military officers, scribes, and government officials. More common people might be merchants or craftspeople. Even within one field, such as crafts-person, one might craft pottery, clothing, or other items for nobles, or just make everyday goods that common people used.

The majority of both men and women worked in farming and food production. Many Mayan men worked in the fields, which was very hard work; they did not have work animals to help them. The Mayas also did not have metal. Their tools were made of stone such as flint or obsidian, a hard volcanic rock that could be as sharp as glass.

Mayan women tended gardens, in which they grew tomatoes, chilies, and herbs, some for cooking and others for use as medicines. Sweet potatoes, manioc, and root vegetables were grown to provide food for the family in the event of a drought, when other crops would not grow.

When Mayan men were not farming, they worked at home in special work areas near their homes, making tools from stone, carving jade, and weaving items such as baskets, rope, and mats, which the Mayas used for sitting on the floor. When a new house needed to be built, or repairs done on existing buildings in their complex, the men worked together.

Mayan weddings symbolized the sacred K'aam Nikté, and was a rite of passage from the secular to the sacred. The ceremony usually took place in a natural setting such as a beach, next to a cenote (say-NOH-

As early as the Pre-Classic period, Mayans built a system of canals and artificial fields. Fish lived in these canals, and canoes could travel on them. The soil the Mayas dredged from the canals was very fertile, and they used it for farming.

Since Mayan homes were built from materials found in the forest, such as wood, adobe, vines, and palm leaves, they needed to be rebuilt or repaired often.

tay; a sinkhole), or forest clearing. The bride wore a white skirt, a colorfully embroidered *huipil* (wedding blouse), and a crown of flowers. The groom and all the guests wore simple white or cream-colored clothing, and everyone was barefoot in order to be closer to nature.

The bride and groom, and the priests who performed the ceremony, stood at the center of the sacred place, which was outlined with rope. They stood before a tree or flowers, which represented

Huipil

the four cardinal points, or the winds that control them. They may also have stood for the four Mayan gods of the cosmos. The tree (Ya'axché, or Tree of Life) represented the regions of darkness, death, illness, and disgrace (the roots); animals, plants, mountains, cenotes, and mankind (trunk); and the heavens (branches).

The ceremony brought together the woman (Mother Earth) and the man (Cosmic Energy), and protected them from the evil spirits that can creep into a home. The priest's words would have been accompanied by music, blowing a conch shell, and burning incense.

When couples were first married, they generally lived with the family of the wife, and the husband worked for the bride's father. Later, they built their own home next door to the home of the wife's parents.

Ix Chel, goddess of childbirth

In addition to cooking, women spent their days cleaning the house, caring for the children, making pottery, tending the garden, spinning thread, and weaving cloth. They made clothing, including loincloths, skirts, and ponchos. Women also made the utensils they used for cooking and other tasks, and helped make necessary repairs on the home, including fixing the thatched roof. They often worked together in communal areas.

Children were the center of the Mayan family, and motherhood was an important job in Mayan society. Women often prayed to the goddess Ix Chel to become pregnant and have an easy childbirth. Men and women also prayed for large families.

Babies and very young children wore no clothing until about four or five years old,

When women were giving birth, the midwife, who may also have been a shaman, was called. An image of Ix Chel was put under the bed, and prayers were said. Babies were bathed as soon as they were born, and were soon brought to the priest by their parents to be named and have their fates told.

when boys were given a loincloth to wear, and girls a skirt. A small white bead was attached by a string to the head of boys when they reached the age of four or five. At this time they would begin training with their fathers. Girls would wear a thin cord with a shell hanging from it around their waists. The shell symbolized their purity.

The Mayas believed a slanting forehead was attractive, and would press a baby's head between two boards when it was an infant and the joints in its skull were still soft. The boards would mold the child's head into the desired shape. They also believed slightly crossed eyes were desirable, so they would hang a small bead on a string from the hair, hanging down between the eyes, which would eventually cause the eyes to cross.

As soon as babies learned to walk, they were allowed to wander and explore their complex. Boys would play with small bows and arrows. Children also played with toy animals made of clay, often in the shape of a jaguar or dog. Though the Mayas never used the wheel for transportation, archaeologists have discovered many Mayan toys with wheels. At the age of anywhere between three and twelve, a ceremony took place called Emku, or the "Descent of God." Bishop De Landa described it as "a thing which has always existed among them and which they hold in such veneration that no one failed to receive it."[3]

During the ceremony, the children were blessed by a priest. A white cloth was placed upon each child's head, and the children were anointed with water mixed with flowers and cacao. Food and wine were offered to the gods, and prayers were said. At the conclusion of the ceremony, the boys' small white beads were cut from their hair, and the cord with the shell was removed from the young girls' waists. At this time, the girls were considered eligible for marriage, whenever their parents wished them to marry. The ceremony was followed by a celebration feast.

For common children, education consisted of an apprenticeship, which taught the child a skill, as well as obedience and respect. Children learned the importance of listening and remaining silent when someone else was speaking, particularly when the speaker was an elder. Schools were attended by children of nobles, and probably only by boys, who lived at them. These schools instructed the students in writing, mathematics, astronomy, religion, the arts, and sports. When children reached adolescence, boys and girls were separated. They were taught what they would need to know as adults, but kept away from the opposite sex until marriage, which usually took place when they were in their teens.

Mayan Cuisine

Though they had no big supermarkets like we do today, the Mayas had a wide variety of foods available to them, from both the plant and animal worlds. The main crops they raised were corn, beans, and squashes. They also grew vanilla and cacao beans, and they sold these to people of the upper classes. The Mayas hunted many types of animals, using simple traps, bows and arrows, spears, and blowguns. Deer, monkeys, crocodiles, turtles, armadillos, many types of birds, and even iguanas were eaten. Fishing offered the Mayas lobster, shrimp, conch, many types of fish, and even manatees.

Mayas had gardens outside their homes, with avocado, pineapple, papaya, guava and other fruit trees, as well as tomatoes, sweet potatoes, and chilies. Women also gathered plants that grew wild in the forests, such as berries.

The staples of most Mayan meals were corn and beans. Women often worked together in communal kitchens and other women's work areas in the complex. Preparing food took up a large part of their time. Maize, the mainstay of the Mayan diet, had to be soaked, peeled, washed, and ground into cornmeal. It was then made into tortillas, which were cooked over a fire. Because the tortillas were best when they were fresh, women cooked them before each meal. They also prepared beans, vegetables, and meats into stews, which were cooked over a hearth. A variety of spices and flavorings, particularly chilies, were added.

Some foods were placed directly on the hot stones to cook, and others, like stews, were cooked in ceramic pots. The Mayas also barbecued meat on skewers, or wrapped the meat in leaves and placed it into a pit with hot stones, then covered the stones with earth.

Mayan tortillas

Cenotes are sinkholes that form where water gradually dissolves the limestone above. Since the Yucatán Peninsula had no rivers and few lakes, these underground bodies of water were extremely important to the cities. Ancient Mayas believed cenotes to be sacred, and sometimes threw valuable objects into them as offerings to the gods.

RELIGION

Chapter 4

Religion was not something the Mayas practiced on just one day of the week, in a place like a church or temple. Rather than being a separate activity, every aspect of their lives was infused with spirituality and their religious beliefs. Many gods existed in the world of the Mayas, and their rulers were believed to be descendants of the gods.

The Mayan religious world had thirteen heavens ruled by sky deities, or gods, and nine underworlds, ruled by the deities of the night. These worlds were positioned between four trees, at the north, south, east, and west corners of the universe. In the center was a fifth tree, the great world tree, which connected the three realms of earth, heaven, and the underworld. They believed the many cenotes that dotted the landscape were underworld entrances.

According to the Mayan creation myth, known as the *Popol Vuh*, the creator gods, Hurakan and Gucumatz, made the earth and the animals, and then attempted to make people to keep count of the days and make offerings to the gods. After unsuccessful attempts to make humans out of mud and wood, the gods finally created human beings from maize, or corn.

THE HERO TWINS

One Hunahpu and his brother Seven Hunahpu were the first generation of Hero Twins, great ballplayers who were defeated by the Lords of Death and sacrificed. One Hunahpu's head was placed by a tree, and when a mortal woman named Blood Woman stopped at the tree and put her hand out, One Hunahpu spat into her hand. From his saliva, the second generation of Hero Twins was born, Hunahpu and Xbalanque.

Through their cleverness and supernatural powers, they managed to defeat the Lords of Death. The Hero Twins then ascended to heaven to become the sun and moon. Their sons became the rulers of the Mayan people on earth. The rulers, in turn, honored their fathers and the sky gods by building ball courts in every town in their world.

Everyday life for the Mayas was overseen by many deities, particularly gods of the sun, rain, and wind, to whom they prayed for protection from the destructive forces of nature, and for the elements needed to provide them with bountiful harvests. The gods could be helpful or destructive, bringing nourishing rain or violent storms, so the Mayas performed rituals throughout the year, made offerings, and said prayers to assure the gods would be benevolent, or kind, to them.

Hunahpu   *Xbalanque*

Religious ceremonies were conducted by priests. Priests purified themselves by fasting before the ceremony began. During the ceremonies, incense was burned, prayers were said, and ritual dances were performed. Animals were often sacrificed, and offerings such as precious stones, feathers, and foods were made to the gods.

Blood was considered a very valuable offering to the gods, and the more important a person was, the more valuable his or her blood was. The blood of rulers and priests was considered most important to offer in order to sustain the gods, but common people probably offered their blood as well. This bloodletting was done by piercing various parts of the body, including the ears, lips, and tongue. Sometimes the blood

Hanal Pixan, an ancient Mayan tradition also known as "supper of the souls," has been celebrated in Mesoamerica since Prehispanic times. Mayas remember those who have passed away and believe they come back to be with their loved ones on these days.

Mayas continue to take part in celebrations for the Mayan New Year. Traditional rituals include fire ceremonies, dances, and ball games. Temples are colored in blue, a sacred color, and new idols are made for worshiping.

was put on paper, which was then burned to send the offering in smoke to the heavenly realms.

Though human sacrifice was known to have been practiced by the Mayas, it is believed it was used only occasionally, most likely during times of severe adversity, such as a drought or famine, or when a ruler was very ill.

The New Year's ceremony was one of the most well known rituals, and is still celebrated by some Mayas today. A direction and a color was associated with each New Year, depending upon which day it began. There was also a new god for the year. An image of the old and new gods were placed facing one another, and then various rituals took place, including the offering of a bird such as a chicken or turkey, the burning of incense, and the building of a frame that represented the four world directions.

Mayan Medicine

Mayan medicine combined spiritual treatments with physical cures consisting of herbal remedies and cleansing, or purification. The ancient Mayas believed that illnesses were caused by the displeasure of the gods, or by an imbalance within the soul. They believed there was no separation of body and spirit, or soul.

If someone was sick, they would consult with the shaman, who was both a priest and a healer skilled in the use of medicinal plants and other types of treatments. The shaman diagnosed a person's illness and prescribed a cure, which would take into consideration the body and mind, including the spirit and the emotions of the patient.

There is evidence that there were both male and female shamans. Some female shamans specialized in rituals and herbs to help women during pregnancy and childbirth. Shamans inherited their knowledge and position from a parent or older relative.

Cures included prayers, as well as medicines derived from plants. Bark from a certain tree was used to help close wounds, and the resin of a particular shrub helped seal damaged blood vessels. A plant known as *Chaya*, or Mayan spinach, was used because of its high protein, iron, and calcium content. Plants were often combined with animal parts from birds, crocodiles, fish, or insects. Some Mayan medicines were mixed into drinks, eaten, smoked, or applied externally as an ointment or plaster.

In addition to medicines, shamans might prescribe fasting or a sweat bath to cleanse impurities. *Pibnas*, or "houses for steaming," were rooms or buildings in which rocks were heated, and then water poured on them, which created steam. Some had separate dressing rooms and areas for relaxing.

The purpose of the steam baths varied. Some were used for health purposes, to cleanse the body and treat certain illnesses and medical conditions, including fevers, poisonous insect and animal bites, and rheumatism. Women used the baths after childbirth. Some sweat baths were built next to ball courts, and were likely used as part of a religious ritual in relation to the ball games. Medicinal herbs were often used in the sweat baths, and cool water was poured over the bathers when they emerged from the bath.

Mayan goddess of healing

Caracol, the observatory at Chichén Itzá in Mexico, is named after the Spanish word for snail. Within its round tower is a staircase, which spirals up like a snail's shell. It is believed that the observatory was built so that astronomers could see the movements of the sun, moon, stars, and planets.

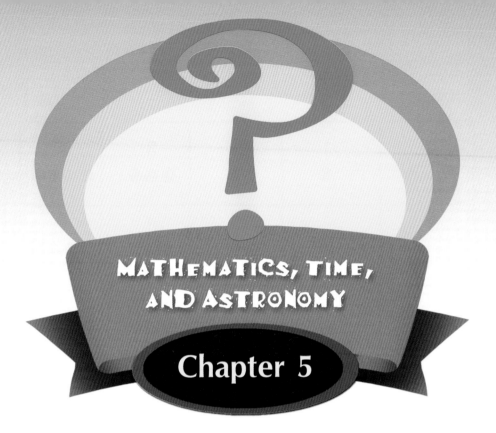

MATHEMATICS, TIME, AND ASTRONOMY

Chapter 5

The Mayan mathematical system was very sophisticated, and the Mayas are believed to be the first civilization to incorporate a symbol for zero into their numerical system. They also used place value.

The Mayan numerical system was called *vigesimal*, or based on the number 20. The base 20 system developed as a result of counting on fingers and toes, which total twenty. *One* was symbolized by a dot, which is believed to be like the tip of one finger. *Five* was written by a bar, like a hand of five fingers stretched out.

The Mayan calendar was used by most of the people in Meso-america, and though its origin remains unknown, names of days were recorded as early as 500 BCE. Some Mayanists believe the calendar may have been first developed by the Olmecs, another group of people who lived in the area.

The purpose of the Mayan calendar was to keep track of the seasons and the cycles of the planets, both of which were thought to be ruled by deities. These cycles repeated, and it was thought that both good and bad events would repeat in the future, just as the cycles repeated.

0 ⭕	1 ●	2 ●●	3 ●●●	4 ●●●●
5 ▬	6 ●/▬	7 ●●/▬	8 ●●●/▬	9 ●●●●/▬
10 ▬▬	11 ●/▬▬	12 ●●/▬▬	13 ●●●/▬▬	14 ●●●●/▬▬
15 ▬▬▬	16 ●/▬▬▬	17 ●●/▬▬▬	18 ●●●/▬▬▬	19 ●●●●/▬▬▬
20 ●/⭕	21 ●/●	22 ●/●●	23 ●/●●●	24 ●/●●●●
25 ●/▬	26 ●/●/▬	27 ●/●●/▬	28 ●/●●●/▬	29 ●/●●●●/▬

The Mayas used a series of dots and bars to signify numbers. A shell symbol signified zero.

The calendars measured days, lunar cycles, solar cycles, seasons, and eclipses, as well as the movement of the planets Mercury, Venus, and Jupiter. Both past and future dates were recorded by Mayan scribes in books or codices, as well as on carved and painted texts and on buildings.

The Mayas had two calendars. The Tzolk'in, or sacred calendar, was 260 days long. This number is thought to correspond with the time from the conception of a child to its birth, and children were thought to have completed one cycle when they were born. They were usually named for the date in the Tzolk'in cycle on which they were born. Shamans planned and oversaw rituals and ceremonies based on the 260-day Tzolk'in calendar.

The second calendar was called the Haab cycle, and was fairly close to our 365-day calendar. It had 360 days, divided into 18 periods of 20 days each. The remaining five days were added to the end of the year, and this time was called Wayeb. Wayeb was a frightening time for the Mayas, as they believed that the portals, or doors between the under-world and earth, were opened then, and the gods could cause destruction for the people. They held rituals during this time in order to prevent disaster, and to prepare for good fortune in the new year.

Later on, the Mayas developed another method of measuring time, called the Long Count because it counted the days from the moment the universe was created. In this system, *k'in* is one day, *winal* one month, and *tun* one year. After 20 *tun*, a *ka'tun* had passed,

Mayan calendar

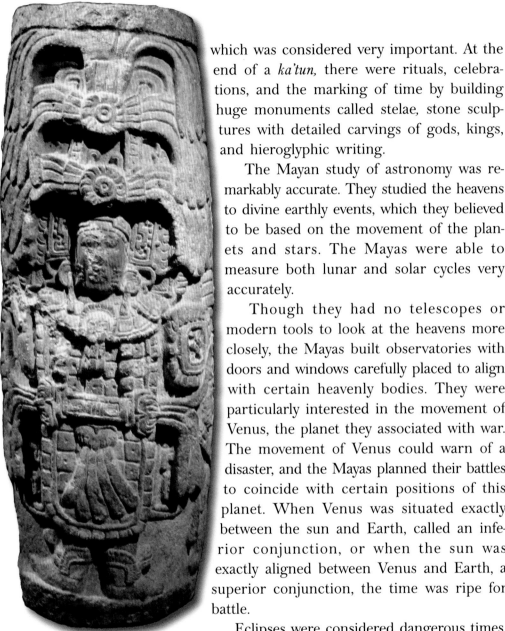

A Mayan stela

which was considered very important. At the end of a *ka'tun,* there were rituals, celebrations, and the marking of time by building huge monuments called stelae, stone sculptures with detailed carvings of gods, kings, and hieroglyphic writing.

The Mayan study of astronomy was remarkably accurate. They studied the heavens to divine earthly events, which they believed to be based on the movement of the planets and stars. The Mayas were able to measure both lunar and solar cycles very accurately.

Though they had no telescopes or modern tools to look at the heavens more closely, the Mayas built observatories with doors and windows carefully placed to align with certain heavenly bodies. They were particularly interested in the movement of Venus, the planet they associated with war. The movement of Venus could warn of a disaster, and the Mayas planned their battles to coincide with certain positions of this planet. When Venus was situated exactly between the sun and Earth, called an inferior conjunction, or when the sun was exactly aligned between Venus and Earth, a superior conjunction, the time was ripe for battle.

Eclipses were considered dangerous times, and solar eclipses were thought to be more dangerous than lunar eclipses. They were referred to as the "biting" of the sun or moon. The Mayas predicted eclipses, and held rituals and ceremonies in order to protect people from the possible disasters that could occur at these times.

FYInfo

Sacred Numbers

Certain numbers were considered sacred by the Mayas. In fact, their mathematical system, as well as their calendars, were all based upon sacred numbers, days, and lengths of time. These numbers were considered critical when predicting events, or when planning ceremonies and rituals. When a child was born, he or she was named according to the birth date. If a child was born on a date that was thought not to be sacred, the child's birthday was simply changed to a luckier day.

Sacred numbers included 4, which symbolized the four directions (north, south, east, and west), as well as 9, which was the number of underworlds in Mayan religion, and 13, which was the number of Mayan heavens, as well as the number of original Mayan gods. The number 5 was considered sacred because it was the number of digits on a human hand or foot, as was 20, because it was the number of fingers and toes combined.

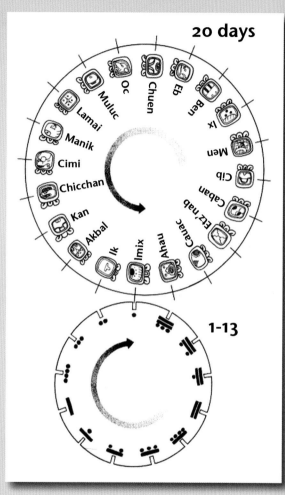

Other sacred numbers were multiples of sacred numbers. A *baktun*, a 400-year cycle, was 20 *ka'tun*, or 20 x 20. The Tzolk'in cycle of 260 days was also made up of two sacred numbers: It was 20 named days paired with 13 numbers, or days. Combining these two numbers resulted in 260 days before the cycle repeated itself.

Sacred numbers were even used in Mayan architecture. In the First Temple at Cerros, built around 50 BCE in Belize, the stairs were built in groups of the sacred numbers 4 and 9. Four stairs led to a landing, and nine steps led to the top of the temple.

Pacal the Great was a Mayan ruler of Palenque, in Mexico, during the Late Classic period. His tomb in the Temple of Inscriptions was discovered in 1948, but it took until 1952 to clear a pathway down the stairs and open it. Whether the skeleton actually belongs to Pacal is a topic of great controversy.

GOVERNMENT

Chapter 6

If you lived in ancient Mayan times, chances are you would have been born as a commoner, for it is thought that commoners made up about 90 percent of the population. However, if you were born into a noble lineage, you would have been a member of the small percentage of the elite. From these lineages emerged rulers, who were also shamans or priests. During the Pre-Classic period, however, there were no kings who ruled over large territories, and the Mayas had not yet begun to organize large projects such as building cities, canals, and reservoirs.

MAYAN MONARCHY

During the Classic period, a central government developed. Whether you lived in a small village or in a city, a king, or possibly a queen, would have ruled from the capital city, and there may have been many cities within the kingdom. The ruler and a small group of wealthy people organized commoners into workforces in order to build public structures, such as temples, roads, canals, and reservoirs. It is possible that government officials who oversaw the smaller cities and towns were part of a developing middle class, which also may have included the lower-ranking priests, artisans, merchants, and soldiers.

At this time, the largest number of people were still commoners, including farmers, laborers, servants, and slaves. Even if you were a commoner, you probably would have lived in a well-built home, and eaten well. In some areas, the commoners and elite had nearly the same material things. The difference between the classes was that the elite could read and had knowledge of religious rituals. Everyone, regardless of rank, was expected to honor the king or queen, and made offerings of both goods and labor.

The Mayas believed that the gods created humans from their own blood. In return, in order to maintain the balance of the universe, Mayan kings and queens offered their blood to the gods during bloodletting ceremonies. Bloodletting was performed by piercing a part of the body.

A stucco relief from Palenque depicting King Upakal K'inich

CRIME AND PUNISHMENT

Under the U.S. democratic government, and according to its legal system, all people accused of a crime are supposed to be treated equally, and given a fair trial and, if found guilty, fair punishment. In ancient Mayan civilization, people were certainly not treated equally in regard to crime and punishment. Punishments varied according to both the crime and the criminal. A crime against a slave, even if it was murder, did not merit the same punishment as a crime against a noble person.

Punishments for nonviolent crimes such as theft, where no one was hurt, were not treated very harshly. For example, a thief who was unable to return what he had stolen could work off his debt, and while he was enslaved for a certain period of time, after he had paid his debt, he was free.

A person who was accused of a crime was brought before the lord of the town or city, who would hear and make a decision regarding the case. The Mayas did not have people who served exclusively as judges; instead, high-ranking officials acted as judges. Spanish missionary Bishop De Landa wrote:

"If they were from the same town, the case was presented before a judge, who acted as an arbiter. After examining the harm done, he ordered satisfaction to be made, and if he were unable to reach a decision on his own, his friends and relations helped him. Such satisfaction was normally demanded for offenses in which someone was killed by accident . . . or when someone was the cause of a fire among the house or arable land, beehives or maize granaries."[4]

While punishment for theft was not unusually harsh, punishment for violent crimes was severe. As Bishop De Landa describes, "offenses committed with intent were always resolved by blood and blows."[5] Murderers were killed in the same way they had killed their victims, or they could be stoned to death, shot with arrows, or dismembered. Death was also the punishment for crimes of attacking women, and for arson, or setting fires.

A chac-mool depicts a human figure reclining with the head up and turned to one side, holding a tray over the stomach. Chac-mools can be found throughout Central Mexico and the Yucatán.

Divine Rulers

Mayan kings and queens were believed to be descendants of the gods, and were responsible for the health, security, and well-being of their kingdoms, which they insured by maintaining a good relationship with the gods.

One such divine ruler was Pacal the Great, also known as Pacal II, who became King of Palenque, in Mexico, in 615. His name means "shield" in Mayan. Pacal succeeded his mother, Lady Zac Kuk, who ruled as queen of Palenque for three years, until Pacal was officially old enough to rule at the age of twelve. His great-grandmother also was a queen of Palenque. Pacal and his oldest son, Chan-Bahlum, or Snake-Jaguar, were responsible for making Palenque into a great power during their reigns.

In the years Pacal was king, during the Classic period, he commissioned buildings that became examples of some of the most impressive and beautiful Mayan architecture ever constructed. Under Pacal's rule, Palenque became what is now regarded as the most beautiful Mayan city-state ever built. One of its buildings was a pyramid called the Temple of Inscriptions, in which Pacal had inscribed on stone slabs a list of the births, accessions, and deaths of all the kings and queens of the Palenque dynasty. This temple also housed the tomb in which it is believed Pacal was buried.

Pacal lived until the age of eighty, and after his death, people worshiped him as a god. It was said that Pacal was able to communicate with his descendants. The Temple of Inscriptions has a stairway down to his tomb, with a long plaster "speaking tube" that led from his sarcophagus to above the ground.

Temple of Inscriptions

The jaguar was a sacred animal to the ancient Mayas. It was associated with power, the underworld, and magical transformations, or the ability to cross between two worlds—the earth and the underworld. The Mayas worshiped a number of jaguar gods and goddesses. Only kings and queens, or very skilled hunters and warriors, were allowed to wear jaguar pelts, teeth, or claws.

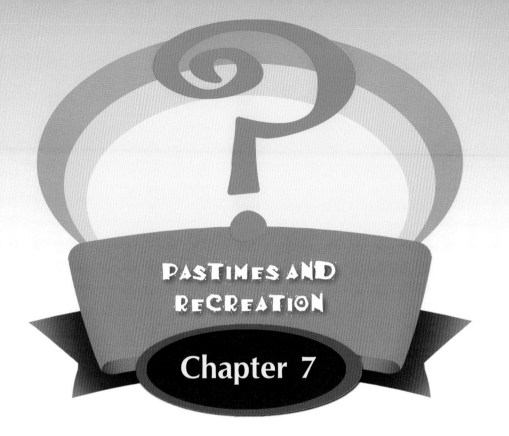

PASTIMES AND RECREATION

Chapter 7

Mayan ceremonies, while religious in nature, also provided a form of entertainment for the people. They were lavish displays that included music, dance, and theatrical performances, as well as feasting, with large amounts of food and drink.

Ceremonies and feasts were held on specific days of religious obligation, which were organized by the rulers and other nobility. Individual families celebrated other occasions, such as weddings and anniversaries of family ancestors.

Music always accompanied ceremonies. Instruments included long thin trumpets made from wood, whistles made from deer bone or shells, reed flutes, and drums. Some drums were held in the hand, and others were beaten with a stick.

Stories such as the creation myth, the *Popol Vuh,* and *Rabinal Achí* were read and performed in public ceremonies, as court dramas. The original pre-Spanish conquest Mayan play *Rabinal Achí (The Man of Rabinal)* tells the history of the Mayas before the European invasion. In the story, a warrior in the service of Lord Five Thunder captures a warrior from the neighboring Quiché tribe, named Cawek of the

Forest People. Cawek is recognized as being a noble and a great warrior, but he is eventually beheaded by the ruler of Rabinal.

When performed traditionally, the actors dance silently, while a chorus sings or chants the dialog of the play. Music is played on long wooden trumpets, which explains the original name of the drama, *Xajoj Tun,* or Dance of the Trumpets.

When the Europeans arrived, they tried to stop these performances, or at least change them into something more Christian. They replaced the Mayan singing with Christian choral music, and suppressed any stories that included human sacrifice.

Dances were of various types, including those in which only one person danced, war dances in which the men participated, and special dances in which only elderly women participated. Most of the time, men and women did not dance together.

At feasts held by nobles, performers included jesters, musicians, and dancers. The jesters were so talented and funny that the Spanish hired them to perform for them, even though the subject of the jesters'

performances included making fun of the Spanish. Large amounts of food were served, including roasted fowl and tamales. There were many varieties of alcoholic drinks, including *balché,* and also drinks made from chocolate.

Games of chance played with dice were popular during ancient Mayan times, and were played by older boys and men. One of the games was called Patolli, which was played on a board similar to a checkerboard. The boards were sometimes made of wood or stone, but could just be carved into the ground. Kernels of corn were marked on one side and used like dice.

Men would gamble, betting their possessions and money. When the stakes became very high, people even bet their own freedom. If they lost, they became a slave to the winner.

The ball game was the best-known game in Mayan times. It may be the first organized sport in human history. The earliest recorded game was played 3,500 years ago, and ruins of ball courts date from as far back as 1400 BCE.

Coba ball court in
Quintana Roo, Mexico

Mayan Fashion

It is clear that the Mayas must have spent a good deal of their spare time adorning themselves with clothing, body art, jewelry, and even decorative dental work. Men of the common class wore relatively simple loincloths, with some embroidery on them, but more important men of the upper classes wore loincloths embellished with colorful embroidery and feathers. Men also wore capelike garments called *patis*, which were made of maguey or cotton, and in the case of nobles, decorated with colorful tail feathers of birds such as quetzals, or made from jaguar or snake skins. *Patis* were also used as blankets.

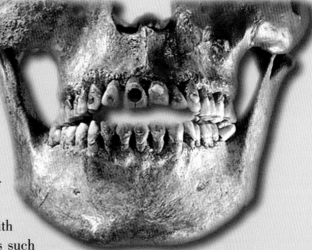

Teeth inlaid with gems

Mayan women's skirts, blouses, and dresses were adorned with embroidery, decorative knots, and fringes. Though men and women often went barefoot, they sometimes wore sandals made of leather or deerskin.

Hair was worn long by both women and men. Generally, hair was worn in a ponytail, or was braided, sometimes with feathers or ribbon. During earlier times, men wore headdresses and women wore turbans, but later, women wore headdresses

Yoke

as well. It is believed that the type of headdress worn indicated a person's position in society.

Jewelry was crafted from shells; bone; semiprecious stones including jade, obsidian, turquoise, amber, and serpentine; and feathers. Necklaces were made from one strand of beads, or collars of several strands. The Mayas also wore bracelets, anklets, and decorative belts. Ears, noses, lips, and cheeks were pierced. Men wore ear plugs, cylinders made of stone or bone that fit through large holes in the earlobes.

Body paint was used to enhance the fierce look of a warrior or the beauty of a woman. Priests wore blue body paint, unmarried men and warriors painted themselves black, married men and women used red. Tattooing was practiced only on married men and women.

Mayan fire dancer in feather headdress

It was considered attractive in Mayan cultures to drill holes into the teeth and insert pieces of decorative stone into the holes. Sometimes the teeth were filed to a point and coated with decorative stone. Though it may seem strange, it is not that different from wearing tooth caps and decorative grills, tooth covers made of metal, a popular hip-hop fashion.

MAKE A MAYAN FOOTED BOWL

As with other types of Mayan crafts, there was a great difference between what was produced for the use of common people and what was made for the nobility. Some craftspeople made pottery for wealthy families. These dishes, pitchers, bowls, and items such as figurines, incense burners, and religious statues were shaped by hand, as all pottery was, because the Mayas had not invented or been introduced to the potter's wheel.

Items for everyday use were made by women in their spare time. Ceramic jars, cooking pots, and griddles were formed using a coil method, wrapping long coils of clay around and around, building it into the desired shape, and then smoothing it out. Clay items were baked, or "fired," in large outdoor ovens.

Mayan pottery was decorated with scenes from daily life, geometric designs, and animals. Some of it was painted with only red, black, and cream-colored paints. Some potters used yellow, orange, and purple as well as blue and green. Ceramics made for the nobility were more colorful than what was made for commoners.

You will need
- Self-hardening clay
- A spray bottle with water or a small bowl or container of water
- A pointed tool such as a chopstick or pencil
- Acrylic paints
- Paintbrush
- Rags or paper towels to clean any accidental spills

Instructions
1. Roll a piece of clay until it is about the size of a Ping-Pong ball, then flatten it into a circle, about ½ inch thick. This will be the base of your bowl.
2. Form clay into "snakes" about ½ inch thick and about 8 or 9 inches long. These snakes, or coils, will become the walls of your bowl.

3. Using your chopstick or pencil point, score the edge of the base by making Xs in the clay. This will help the coil stick to the base better.

4. Moisten your fingers with water, and rub the outside edge of your base to wet the clay. This will create a wet, sticky clay called slip. This will glue your coils together. Wrap your coil along the edge of the base, and continue wrapping it around, building up the walls of your bowl. Score the top edge of each coil, and moisten the clay into slip before you place the next coil on top. You can use as many coils as you like, pressing the ends together, until your bowl is the size you want it to be.

5. Once your bowl is built, wet the sides with your spray bottle, and with your fingers, smooth the sides until they are flat, on the inside and outside of the bowl, until you can't see the coils.

6. To make the foot, repeat steps 1–5, making a much smaller bowl shape.

7. Score the bottom of both bowls, wet the scored areas to create slip, and with your bowl upside down, attach the foot, smoothing the clay with your fingers to cover the seams between the bowl and the foot.

8. If you want to, you can engrave designs into your bowl before it dries.

BCE

11,000	First people settle in the Mayan highlands and lowlands.
3114	The world is created, according to Mayan calendar.
2600	Mayan civilization begins to form.
2000	Peak of the Olmec civilization.
1800	Start of the Pre-Classic period.
700	Writing develops in Mesoamerica.
300	Mayan society is ruled by nobles and kings. Mayan cities Tikal, Uaxactún, Abaj Takalik, Dzibilchaltún, El Mirador, Cerros, Acanceh, and Maní are created.

CE

100	The Olmec civilization declines.
250	The Classic period starts.
300	Cities along the Usumacinta River, Yaxchilán, Kaminaljuyu, and Piedras Negras are built.
500	Tikal becomes the first great Mayan city.
600	Tikal becomes the largest Mayan city, with as many as 500,000 inhabitants.
751	Long-standing Mayan alliances begin to break down. Trade between Mayan city-states declines, and interstate conflict increases.
800	Toltecs invade Chichén Itzá, signaling the beginning of the end for the southern cities as they go into major decline. Many are abandoned.
899	Tikal is abandoned.
900	Classic period ends with the collapse of the southern lowland cities. Maya cities in the northern Yucatán continue to thrive. The Post-Classic period begins.
976	Mayan tradition becomes mixed with Toltec tradition.
1194	After conflict between Chichén Itzá, Uxmal, and Mayapán, Chichén Itzá is destroyed.
1200	Mayas begin to abandon their northern cities.
1511	Spaniards are shipwrecked on the eastern shore of Yucatán.
1517	The Spanish, under Hernández de Córdoba, arrive on the shores of Yucatán. With the Spanish come smallpox, influenza, and measles, which will kill 90 percent of Mesoamerica's native populations before 1600.
1519	Hernán Cortés begins exploring Yucatán.
1541	The Spanish are finally able to put an end to Maya resistance, but Tayasal, the last functioning Maya city, remains independent until 1697.
1542	The Spanish establish a capital city at Mérida in Yucatán.

CHAPTER NOTES

All quotes in this book were taken from A.R. Pagden's *The Maya: Diego de Landa's Account of the Affairs of Yucatán* (Chicago: J. Philip O'Hara, Inc., 1975).

1. p. 43.
2. p. 70.
3. p. 76.
4. p. 72.
5. Ibid.

FURTHER READING

Books

Braman, Arlette. *Secrets of Ancient Cultures: The Maya–Activities and Crafts from a Mysterious Land.* Hoboken, N.J.: John Wiley & Sons, 2003.

Coulter, Laurie. *Ballplayers and Bonesetters: One Hundred Ancient Aztec and Maya Jobs You Might Have Adored or Abhorred.* New York: Annick Press, 2008.

Day, Nancy. *Your Travel Guide to Ancient Mayan Civilization.* Minn., Minnesota: Runestone Press, 2001.

Harris, Nathaniel. *Ancient Maya: Archaeology Unlocks the Secrets of the Maya's Past.* Washington, D.C.: National Geographic Society, 2008.

Jolley, Dan. *The Hero Twins Against the Lords of Death: A Mayan Myth.* Minneapolis, Minn.: Lerner Publications, 2008.

Works Consulted

Benson, Elizabeth. *The Maya World.* New York: Thomas Y. Crowell, 1967.

Coe, Michael. *The Maya.* Seventh Edition. New York: Thames & Hudson, 2005.

Coe, Michael, and Justin Kerr. *The Art of the Maya Scribe.* New York: Harry N. Abrams, 1998.

Coe, Michael, and Rex Koontz. *Mexico: From the Olmecs to the Aztecs.* New York, Thames & Hudson, 2002.

Foster, Lynn V. *Handbook to Life in the Ancient Mayan World.* New York: Facts on File, Inc., 2002.

Henderson, John S. *The World of the Ancient Maya.* Ithaca, New York: Cornell University Press, 1997.

Houston, Stephen, and Takeshi Inomata. *Royal Courts of the Ancient Maya: Theory, Comparison, and Synthesis.* Volume 1. Boulder, CO: Westview Press, 2001.

Pagden, A.R. *The Maya: Diego de Landa's Account of the Affairs of Yucatán.* Chicago: J. Philip O'Hara, Inc., 1975.

Phillips, Charles. *The Illustrated Encyclopedia of Aztec & Maya.* London: Lorenz Books, 2004.

——. *The Mythology of the Aztec & Maya.* London: Southwater, 2006.

Rome, Jesus. *The Civilization of the Maya.* New York: Crescent Books, 1980.

Sabloff, Jeremy A. *The New Archaeology and the Ancient Maya.* New York: Scientific American Library, 1990.

Schele, Linda, and David Freidel. *A Forest of Kings: The Untold Story of the Ancient Maya.* New York: William Morrow & Co., 1990.

On the Internet

Guatemala: Cradle of the Maya
Civilization
http://www.authenticmaya.com

The Jaguar Sun: Maya People of the
Past and Present
http://www.jaguar-sun.com/maya.
html

Mayan Kids
http://www.mayankids.com/

NOVA Online: Lost King of the Maya
http://www.pbs.org/wgbh/nova/maya/

Science Museum of Minnesota: Maya
Adventure
http://www.smm.org/sln/ma/
index.html

The Sport of Life and Death: The
Mesoamerican Ballgame
http://www.ballgame.org

*A statue representing
a wealthy Mayan man*

assimilated (ah-SIM-ih-layt-ed)—To take in as one's own.

codex (KOH-dex)—A primitive book; the plural is codices (KOH-deh-seez).

commission (kuh-MIH-shun)—To place an order for.

communal (kuh-MYOO-nul)—Shared by a group.

drought (DROUT)—A long period of dry weather.

hacha (HAT-chuh)—A decorative stone accessory worn on a ballplayer's yoke, often carved in the shape of an animal.

hieroglyphics (hy-roh-GLIH-fiks)—A type of writing using figures or symbols.

jade—A green mineral used as a gemstone.

loincloth—A piece of cloth worn around the hips to cover private parts.

maracas (mah-RAH-kahs)—Gourds that have been filled with seeds, used as musical rattles.

mason (MAY-sun)—A person who builds with stone or bricks.

Mesoamerica (met-zoh-uh-MAYR-ih-kuh)—The area extending from central Mexico to Honduras and Nicaragua in which pre-Columbian civilizations flourished.

Olmecs (OHL-meks)—A Mesoamerican civilization that thrived from c.1000 to 400 BCE along the southern Gulf coast of Mexico; they had extensive agriculture, a calendar system, long-distance trade networks, pyramids, ceremonial centers, and very fine jade work.

palma—A decorative stone accessory worn on a ballplayer's yoke; it had the shape of a palm leaf.

plaza (PLAH-zuh)—A public square or open space in a city or town.

resin (REH-zin)—Any of numerous clear or translucent, yellowish or brownish substances that ooze from certain trees and plants.

sarcophagus (sar-kah-FAH-gus)—A stone coffin.

scribe—A professional writer.

shaman (SHAH-mun)—A person who acts as a go-between for the natural and supernatural worlds.

stela (STEEL-uh)—An upright stone or slab with an inscribed or sculptured surface, used as a monument.

yoke—A piece of a garment that is closely fitted, either around the neck and shoulders or at the hips, and from which an unfitted or gathered part of the garment is hung.

Effigy urn in the likeness of the Mayan sun god

ABOUT THE AUTHOR

Elizabeth Scholl writes educational books and magazine articles for children and young adults, specializing in social studies and science topics. She has a background in education, and was a classroom teacher for over fifteen years. Elizabeth greatly enjoyed exploring history with her students, and devoted a lot of time to learning about the lifestyles of ancient civilizations and indigenous cultures such as the Mayas. When she is not writing, she enjoys reading, gardening, visiting museums and historical sites, bicycling, and spending time outdoors. She lives in northern New Jersey with her husband, three children, dog, and two very mischievous orange cats.